Published by

www.elisabeth-lukas-archiv.de

© 2024 Elisabeth-Lukas-Archiv gGmbH
Dr. Heidi Schönfeld
Nürnberger Straße 103a
D-96050 Bamberg
info@elisabeth-lukas-archiv.de

This English edition was originally published in German as
In der Trauer lebt die Liebe weiter Butzon & Bercker, 2021

Elisabeth Lukas, Love lives on in grief

Translated from the German by:
Dr. David Nolland, Oxford

Cover, typesetting, layout and image editing:
Bernhard Keller, Cologne

Print and distribution: tredition, Hamburg
ISBN: 978-3-384-21037-1

Elisabeth Lukas

Love lives on in grief

LIVING LOGOTHERAPY

A publication series of the Elisabeth-Lukas-Archive

Contents

Grief is more than a feeling

Grief is by no means simply a feeling, even a feeling of misery. Feelings can be produced by artificial means, for example with the help of drugs or psychoactive substances or by electrically stimulating certain parts of the brain. Feelings can be dampened or even suppressed by means of desensitisation, routine, or manipulation, or by the cutting of neural pathways. Feelings are inner states that come and go, sometimes in step with external events, sometimes not. Experiments on animals show that a chicken in a cage can be made to feel angry, hungry, sleepy or sexually aroused within fifteen minutes by administering the right stimuli. Humans could be made to respond in a similar way.

Grief is different. It lies deep in the heart, at the spiritual centre of the person, and cannot be either summoned or driven off. It is much more than a feeling, it is an awareness of something valuable having been lost. Nothing can erase this awareness. Even sedatives cannot prevent this awareness from being present in every waking moment. Likewise, nothing can undo the loss. Attempting to replace the person who has been lost with anything else only serves to emphasise their irreplaceability. Nothing can make the lost treasure less precious.

The pain of loss burns the value of what has been lost into the consciousness. The awareness of loss accompanies the bereaved person through life, like a whispering voice that may sometimes be louder, sometimes less loud, but which cannot be silenced, always speaking wistfully of what used to be so precious.

Yes, the griever is aware of much. But strangely this inescapable awareness of loss can be the key to coping with the resulting suffering. It opens a series of doorways to new dimensions of awareness. By passing through these doorways, the griever is changed, and so are his or her emotions. Grief is a journey towards a new, more clear-sighted mode of human existence. In this book we will follow this pain-induced journey step by step.

Grief is a reflection of wealth

The first gateway to be crossed, after the immediate awareness of loss, is the realisation that there has been something of great value present in one's life. This immediate insight in the face of tragedy already contains a grain of consolation. One's life has not been empty – one has not languished in solitude. One has lived in relationship with others, and the most interesting of these relationships have been ones of love. It is good to remind oneself of this and to reaffirm it.

Why is it good? Another important realisation: we humans have a problematic tendency to take wealth for granted – even inner wealth. As soon as someone precious enters into our life: a romantic partner, a friend, or a child, we get used to treating them as a possession to which we have an automatic right. Soon, we no longer even notice how much our existence is enriched and intensified by these people to whom we are bound. We only remember their value and significance when they have departed. Grief puts a red pencil through all these absurd ideas of entitlement. Everything is on loan, everything is a gift – life itself is a gift up to the moment of death – this is what is written in the place of all our deleted fantasies of possession. But grief also tells us: Look! You were one of the lucky recipients. These gifts were bestowed upon you for years. Now this is the price you have to pay. The more intimate your love, the happier you were, the more bitterly you will weep over the loss of the joy you were granted.

Once, at a scientific conference in Dallas, I took part in a sightseeing tour for foreign speakers. The bus tour took us past some of the most magnificent gardens and the most expensive houses in America. The tour guide told us how many millions of dollars had been invested in each of them. When he enthused about a particularly impressive mansion with gutters made of pure gold, I made the succinct remark:

"But this is all just on loan." The tour guide looked at me with annoyance: "Are you trying to scare me?"

It was not at all my intention to scare him. But I felt sorry for him that he was so shaken by this comment. Life will eventually run its red pencil through his fantasies as well...

Wealth does not consist of an overabundance of things that will have to be left behind. True wealth consists of a full life – a life of devotion to many wonderful treasures. The loss of these treasures will have to be grieved when they are taken away. Grief is a re-flection of wealth.

Those who are truly poor are those who have nothing to grieve over. They have nothing to lose because there is nothing that quickens their heart. These are the poorest people of all.

Can love die?

Like grief, love is not just a feeling. It is certainly not a feeling of dependence or blind subservience from the wastes of a sick soul. True love has nothing to do with low self-worth and a resultant desire to lean on someone more solid. The use or misuse of other people for selfish purposes is foreign to it. It does not seek a partner for protection or stimulation, it does not want a poster child for the curation of its own image, and it does not crave praise and tenderness for self-gratification. Love demands nothing at all; it is sovereign. The 'substance' from which it is made is a simple, unconditional yes to the beloved person – like a shooting star from the fireworks of creation. As Strauss put it in his operetta *The Gypsy Baron,* love is a "heavenly force".

Thus, love can do whatever is necessary: leave the other person alone, let them go, release them if need be with moist eyes but an honest heart. Time moves on, but love remains. Feelings may fade, but love endures. Death dissolves obligations, but love remains. How could an unconditional yes turn into a no just because of a change of circumstances? What if the other person changes course, falls ill, moves away, or dies? The part of a mutual relationship that was truly love survives even the end of the relationship.

But in what form does it survive? Well, that is not hard to work out. In a joyful resonance with the being and essence of the other person. In not forgetting them. In praying for them. And – in silent mourning for them. Grief says: "I am the price to be paid for your values. I am a reflection of your wealth. In me, your love is immortal."

Viennese psychiatrist Viktor E. Frankl expressed this poignantly in his book The Doctor and the Soul, p 108

"Consider, for instance, the affects of grief and repentance. From the utilitarian point of view, both must necessarily appear to be meaningless. To mourn for anything irrevocably lost must seem useless and

foolish from the point of view of "sound common sense"[...] But for the inner history of man, grief [... does] have meaning. Grieving for a person whom we have loved and lost in a sense continues his life [...] The loved person whom we grieve for has been lost objectively, in empirical time, but he is preserved subjectively, in inner time." (Quotation shortened.)

Remembrance that leads to freedom

Many ways of looking back make one unfree. Psychotherapy knows a thing or two about this. In the exuberance of its youth (as a scientific discipline, psychotherapy has only been around for about 150 years), it has done much damage with its unqualified promotion of retrospection. Quite a few patients who only needed a bit of encouragement have become bogged down in the psychoanalytical process with the memorisation of negative childhood events and have never been able to break free from this. Throughout their lives, they have felt determined and influenced by past horrors.

Looking back with reproach makes one unfree. The reproach, whether towards oneself or others, hangs on one's chest in the form of a gnawing resentment, and is carried forward as historical "excess baggage". Closely related is looking back with despair. The patterns of thought: "if only …" or "if only I had …"

are stultifying companions, stumbling along behind the departed train of events. Looking back with dissatisfaction is also unconstructive. The question, 'What have I gotten out of my life?' is almost impossible to ask without a complaining or accusing tone. The answer, "not much...nothing at all," leads seamlessly to looking back with bitterness. Paradoxically, the opposite answer can also lead to paralysis. Looking back with rose-tinted glasses, dreaming of a romanticised past, nails the present firmly to what has long vanished.

Grief, aware of a precious – though limited – gift that it mourns, and in which love lives on (as it grieves for the beloved), can find more constructive perspectives. For example, it can look back with gratitude. This is an incomparable way to sooth wounds, alleviate pain, and bring peace! Or, it can look back as an artist. Every artist must step back from a work of art before finishing it, to view, judge, and perfect it from a distance. Whatever field they work in, they must, like a painter stepping back from their easel, obtain an overall impression of what they have created. Only then can they see the tiny details that need improvement in the interest of the whole. In the same way, people should occasionally look back on their life from a spatial and temporal distance to recognise meaningful additions that are still to be made. In this sense, a time of grief can inspire the application of artistic "final touches". For example, in the case of a death, we might take care of the deceased person's effects, or modify our actions and attitudes in line with their wishes.

In 1870, the Norwegian poet Henrik Ibsen wrote to Laura Kieler: "Spiritually, man is a farsighted creature – we see most clearly from a great distance... Summer is best described on a winter day." His words could also be expressed in this way: "The happiness we have experienced is best appreciated in grief."

If this succeeds, it opens the way to the most liberating perspective of all: looking back with blessing. Here, we trust in "higher connections of meaning", approving of what has been; the beautiful alongside the less beautiful, with all its beginnings and endings. The Lord giveth, the Lord taketh away, blessed be the name of the Lord ...

Resurrection from grief

The mental process we have described goes hand in hand with a number of specific healing processes. Probably nature, which arranges things very wisely, spreads the dark veil of grief over a misfortune so that the person affected can recover under its protection. The healing processes are as follows:

1. Retreat into silence
2. Facing the situation
3. Carving out a liveable situation
4. Heightened spirituality

1. It is often observed that people who are grieving shield themselves from the encouraging words of others. When there is no possible consolation, all words are superfluous. Those who have not experienced something similar cannot really speak about it. Well-meant attempts at reassurance by

friends can be rather annoying. One wants to be polite, but not to be fobbed off with clichés, and it is difficult to express both sentiments at the same time. Human company is welcome, but only if it does not cause pain. Probing the pain too deeply can touch a nerve.

A grandmother whose 38-year-old daughter had died in a traffic accident along with her two preschool children told me that she could not bear the sympathy of her village community. Every half-curious and half-embarrassed glance she received and every stammered question about how she was doing stirred up the pain in her soul. She preferred an old, undaunted friend. This friend would often come to visit, bringing a homemade cake. She would drink coffee and chat about trivialities. She would help with the dishes, and if she saw freshly dried laundry in the bathroom, she would immediately pick up an iron. When she came to say goodbye, she would hug her without comment. The grandmother added that her friend had also been through difficult times, but she didn't flaunt it; instead, she demonstrated her will to live through her actions, and that was almost contagious. This simple, practical friendship helped her more than anything else.

The solitude into which grieving people tend to retreat, almost like wounded animals, is a reservoir of silence for recharging. No reservoir is designed for constant consumption. A water reservoir, for example, exists to get us through periods of drought. When there is enough water, there is no need to tap into it. Similarly, silence and solitude get us through periods of existential crisis, but they are not permanent companions. Thrown back on the self, an individual regroups around their core. After an initial outburst, after the crying and sobbing, they settle into an inner calm. They can still hardly fathom what has happened, but the silence is patient. It compels no response. The person can gently approach the unfathomable, extending or retracting their feelers as they are able. "It hurts so much," they lament in their grief. "Give me your pain," the silence responds, "I will absorb it."

2. After the calm settles, mental engagement with the altered situation begins. This is easier if it can be anchored to what is familiar. Loss will certainly have had to be dealt with in the past. How was it then? The world did not collapse. Life still offered new, meaningful tasks. For as long as one is here on Earth, there is something important to be done, and that is no different now. Grief is no excuse to shirk one's responsibilities. Admittedly, the altered situation necessitates some serious adjustments. But creativity keeps the soul elastic. Throughout the ages, people have crafted their sorrows into heroic acts; how much vitality has arisen from the blows of fate they suffered! And how much were they lured into lethargy and convenience by the sunny side of life! So, pull your head out of the sand and face the demands of the moment! What is required of you right now – in, because of, or despite your grief ... ?

The grandmother we mentioned could remember the exact day on which she woke up from her emotional petrification. Within the solitude of her four walls, her next task became clear to her: she needed to take care of her son-in-law. After the sudden death of his wife and two children, he was on the verge of collapse. During the day, he had to focus on his job, which was challenging enough. But he wasted his evenings drifting through bars. The grandmother pulled herself together and contacted him. After weeks of effort, she succeeded in convincing him to lead a better life. Flipping through the family photo album, she nodded reassuringly at the last photo of her daughter, as if to say: "Your husband is okay." She felt that the picture smiled back at her, saying, "Thank you, Mum!"

3. Once the grieving person has found his way back to him or herself and the tasks awaiting in the silence, the most difficult part of the cognitive process begins. Answers must be found to the questions that press insistently on all sides. To do this, however, wrongly posed questions must first be weeded out, questions like: "Why did this happen to me?", "What am I being punished for?", "What is the meaning of my suffering?", "Why didn't God stop this from happening?" These questions are wrongly posed because they assume that the ways of Providence can be understood by our limited minds. A sparrow might as well question the purpose of the high-voltage line on which it is sitting. It is not that the line is without purpose – it is just impossible to try to explain it to a sparrow.

Some people are constantly preoccupied by these wrong questions. Questions like: "Who is to blame for my dilemma?" and "Why doesn't anyone help me?" are real traps. Psychotherapeutic methodology will often attempt to redirect such questions into: "What good can come out of having experienced this?",

"What can I learn from it?", "How can I best deal with it?", "Can an inner triumph be forged from this tragedy?" These are exciting questions. They elicit great answers from the people who ask them. Answers with which one can live and go on living.

The grandmother also found answers and defined her position in the face of the great misfortune that had robbed her of her loved ones. She said to me: "I had a healthy and able daughter for thirty-eight years. I never questioned why she was healthy and able. I never questioned why she wasn't born sick or dead; why she didn't fail at school or develop poorly. Everything was just great. So I can't argue about it now. Perhaps her early death has a meaning that I cannot understand." Hesitating, she continued: "I cannot understand at all ehy my two grandchildren had to die so early. When I think about how eagerly they were awaited ... Well, at least they were spared the horrors of this world. They passed from the bosom of the family to the bosom of the Creator without suffering, without sorrow, without being compromised in any way ..." Tears streamed down her cheeks, but she wiped them away decisively. "I'm still learning to allow them their heavenly peace," she whispered, "I'm still learning."

4. Ultimately, viable answers can only come from faith, where the word "faith" here is meant in a universal rather than a specifically religious sense. Everyone begins by believing in something (someone?) higher than themselves. It is a denial of their original character if, in intellectual arrogance, they elevate themselves to the highest pinnacle of being. However, borderline experiences and times of mourning melt away this kind of arrogance. A return to faith is comforting and beneficial to health.

The biochemist Caryle Hirshberg[1] (Ben Lomond, USA) studied unexpected remission in people with advanced cancer. In around fifty different patients who should have long since fallen victim to their illness, according to medical reports, she determined three consistent behavioural factors:

1. The patients accepted their diagnosis, but not their prognosis, that is, they were optimistic in spite of their diagnosis.

2. They had stable social relations; over seventy percent of them had been married for more than twenty years.

3. They *prayed*.

If an intensification of one's own spirituality can help in a fight against cancer, then surely it can also contribute to a resurrection from grief.

Tolerating ignorance

When we discussed withdrawal into silence, we mentioned that the intended encouragements of others do not always produce the desired effect. People who are close to the grieving person and sense their immense pain are especially likely to feel that they need to find some way to help them. Though they half-realise that nothing can be done – at least not with verbal assurances, the temptation to try anyway is all the greater if people are socially outgoing and charitably minded. That's why sometimes it is the most truly caring people who make a mistake and incur the displeasure of the grieving person. Long-standing friendships have been destroyed when one person has been devastated by tremendous suffering and the other has desperately wanted to provide consolation.

The crux of the matter is that our empathy is invariably limited. We cannot truly and completely understand another person. We cannot slip into their shoes and fully understand their emotional responses. As each person is an individual, they perceive their fate individually. Furthermore, their fate is one that is not ours, it is alien to us unless we have experienced something similar. This is why similar experiences connect people with each other. But even similar experiences only resemble each other at the level of external events and not in how they are lived through by the people affected. We are all separated by a certain degree of foreignness.

At a disability fair I once saw experiments that were supposed to help reduce the gap in understanding between disabled and non-disabled people. Relatives and interested parties were strapped with devices that allowed them to experience how shaky and uncontrolled an MS patient's movements are or how difficult paralysis on one side makes it to speak and walk. Meanwhile, other visitors were given black glasses that shut out every glimmer of light, given mobility canes and asked to cover a short distance without help. These activities were extremely educational for the able-bodied. Some of the relatives may be much more patient with their disabled family member in the future ...

There is a flip side to this coin. Disabled people also need to be patient with their non-disabled compatriots when they behave in a clumsy way. In 95% of these cases, people don't want to cause offense, but simply don't understand any better due to a lack of empathy. Likewise, grieving people are advised to be tolerant of unhelpful offers of support. They may have to hear that nothing is as bad as it seems, that time heals all wounds, or that these things have happened to other people. Even Viktor E. Frankl, who was truly mentally robust, had to grit his teeth when, after years of torture in German concentration camps during World War II, in which most of his family perished and he himself was on the brink of death, he was told with a shrug: "We also suffered."

This throwaway comment wasn't even wrong, it was just extremely insensitive. Of course, there was widespread suffering. One should never measure one instance of suffering against another, because they are incommensurable. Soldiers on the front experienced terrible things, women and children suffered in the bombed-out hinterland. There was so much hardship in Vienna after the war that there was not enough room to give adequate compassion to the former inmates of the concentration camps. Viktor E. Frankl was generous enough to forgive. And all grieving people should be equally generous. One should be careful not to react too sensitively to the inconsiderateness of those who do not understand. It is important to keep three things in mind: 1. These insensitive people don't mean badly – in most cases they mean well. 2. They cannot adequately imagine what is going on inside the grieving person. They shouldn't be blamed for that – they are simply ignorant. 3. Those who are grieving are also unable to empathize fully with people in completely different situations who are suffering.

Let us therefore all take note: For all of us there is an ultimate solitude in which we stand alone – before ourselves? – before God?

Release from fear

There are difficulties that interfere with health-restoring grief work. Often, they have nothing to do with the bereavement itself, but rather with the temperament of the grieving person. Hypersensitivity is one such difficulty that is attributable to an anxious ("nervous") temperament. In technical language, it manifests itself in a "disproportionate organismic response to stimulation, combined with unrealistic spontaneous interpretations." The problem, to put it simply, involves an excessive reaction to small things (for example, there may be a physical response, such as trembling, sweating, or diarrhoea) and premature expectation of negative, threatening outcomes. A father's children want to light a campfire in the park, and he immediately anticipates a disastrous fire. Without investigating how safe the fireplace is, he peremptorily dismisses the children's plans. A woman has to brake suddenly because a truck swerves in front of her and she is left in shock for hours. Instead of being relieved that no damage was done, she is unable to stop contemplating the terrible accident that almost occurred. Another man suffers from frequent spasms resulting in unclear speech. A police officer he asks for information thinks he is drunk. Although the officer apologizes after the mistake is explained, the man is offended for days by the cruelty of fellow human beings whose perceived purpose is nothing but humiliation.

An anxious temperament produces an automatic violent reaction to relatively harmless events: as soon as they occur, they are experienced as stressful and personally threatening. This response involves both emotional and cognitive processes: the anxious person dramatizes the undramatic and anticipates drama, which exacerbates fear.

A contrasting example is a woman who was attacked on a forest path. Suddenly there were quick footsteps behind her, and before she could turn around, a man wrapped strong arms around her waist from behind.

Her initial reaction was to think about who in her circle of friends might be playing a trick on her. "Shall I guess who you are?" she called, turning around. The man didn't answer and tried to force her into the bushes. Then she realised what was happening and kicked out so hard that the attacker gave up his plan and fled.

Understandably, people whose initial reactions – the spontaneous reactions that cannot be controlled voluntarily – are invariably fearful, are disadvantaged in life. However, they can practice correcting their gloomy worldview with reality checks. The anxious father can mentally arrive at the perspective that on countless occasions children have lit a campfire in the park, sat and sung around it, and had an enjoyable evening. There is a high probability that nothing bad will happen this time either. Similarly, the startled driver can come up with a more reasonable perspective: "I've been driving for eight years now without any accidents and have just shown that I can handle even tricky driving situations skilfully. Also,

there must be a guardian angel watching over me ..."
In the same way, the speech-impaired person can reduce his anger: "It is understandable that my slurred speech can be confused with drunkenness. I don't have a sign hanging around my neck explaining my illness, and the people around me are not clairvoyant! So I can forgive the officer for his clumsy words."

Reality is infinitely bigger and more diverse than it appears to a fearful person. It contains thousands of strokes of luck, near misses, undeserved kindnesses and gracious acts. Admittedly, there are also dark hours. But anyone who only sees the darkness is fundamentally mistaken.

If a serious loss is suffered by a person with an anxious disposition who has always groped through the darkness with nightmares and tendencies to panic, two things can happen. The first possibility is the person will feel this as a confirmation of a negative world view and this view will be reinforced. No one will ever again be able to bring them into the light. The second possibility is that they may finally understand that unnecessary fears have not protected them from the blows of fate but have only prevented them from being satisfied with normal everyday life and its small joys. This can bring about a change of perspective.

"The crowning experience of all, for the home-coming man, is the wonderful feeling that, after all he has suffered, there is nothing he need fear anymore – except his God.," wrote Viktor E. Frankl after his liberation from the concentration camp[2]: People who can speak in this way have learned an infinite amount from their grief.

A metaphor from zoology can support these ideas. As everyone knows, a caterpillar spins itself into a cocoon to emerge as a butterfly after its meta-morphosis. It is extremely difficult to escape the cocoon. The young butterfly has to apply enormous force to break open the hard shell of the cocoon with its delicate wings.

Scientists were curious to see what would happen if the butterfly received assistance. At the appropriate time, they artificially opened a series of cocoons from the outside. The young butterflies crawled out unharmed, but they didn't fly. Not a single one of them took to the skies. Because they couldn't collect any flower nectar, they starved to death.

The effort to break free of the cocoon is necessary, so that the animals learn to trust the strength of their wings. Without this experience of working on their own, they do not dare to leave the "safe" ground. How reminiscent this is of some people who do not dare to live their own life. A period of grief could be a metamorphosis after which they succeed in breaking through the tight shell of fear with their spiritual wings.

Reparation for guilt

So far, we have considered grief that comes with knowing that something precious has been lost. It is grief with two faces: one that is radiant about the gift that has been received, and one that is sad about its temporary and finite nature. In contrast to this, there is grief with only one face. It does not weep for a blessed treasure that is gone, but rather for a failure to actualise its value.

Who hasn't experienced grief about bad decisions that they have made and can never change? Who hasn't experienced gnawing remorse for careless or stupid actions taken and later regretted? Very few of us ever intend anything malicious – although we often attribute evil intentions to those who are close to us. But no, most of us weren't aiming for consequences which are contrary to meaning, and we certainly weren't trying to miss opportunities for meaning. We were simply shy, indolent, tired, hesitant, awkward ...

at the wrong moment; and the decisive moment was lost.

None of this matters if reparations can be made. An acknowledgement of our mistake, a frank discussion or a decent confession clears things up. A show of goodwill alone can smooth over many a controversy. But what can ease the soul's pain when reparation is not possible, for example, because the person you have wronged is no longer alive? Grief still has both its faces, but one of them is poorer than the other because it can no longer claim to reflect only wealth. Things that went wrong and opportunities that were missed are also reflected in it. Nevertheless, love lives on even in this type of grief, and I would like to illustrate this with an example.

A father lost his little daughter. During the re-modelling of their house, she fell unnoticed into a vat of lime water and drowned. The father tore himself apart with self-reproach because he had not covered the tub with boards or a protective tarp.

I told him about one of my early childhood memories. One summer afternoon, my mother had tied her watch around my wrist and allowed me to go to the nearby park to play ball. I was supposed to be home again at 6 p.m. At 4 p.m. the watch stopped. I ran around without realising, and since the hands of the watch never reached 6 p.m., I didn't go home. Finally, it began to get dark, which seemed strange to me, and I finally returned home. It was just as strange that my father, who was usually never home before 8 p.m., opened the door. As soon as he saw me, he started beating me around the ears. I didn't understand what was going on. My mother mumbled that it was too late for dinner and sent me to bed. Even after these clear signs, I could find no explanation for the strange events. I washed myself, put down my mother's watch and crawled under the covers.

Suddenly the light came on in my bedroom and my parents appeared at my bedside. They knelt down and apologised. (Apparently, they had discovered the broken watch and deduced the reason for my lateness.) My mother had brought some warm soup. My father confessed to losing his temper. Out of concern for me, he emphasised. He had been terribly upset because I had been missing for so long, he had wanted to call in a police search, etc. I will never forget that hour: I enjoyed the situation massively, it surpassed my wildest dreams. Being allowed to eat soup in bed and having my father on his knees before me ... It was like having my birthday and Christmas at the same time!

"Your parents are to be envied," exclaimed the grieving father when I had finished. "They were able to make amends for their mistake. But what should I do?" "Exactly the same thing," I answered, "with one unimportant difference. You will do it in your imagination. Visit your daughter in a place where you feel close to her. Stay there, close your eyes and let an image of her form before you. Then ask your daughter if you can apologise for leaving the tub uncovered and let yourself be surprised by her response."

The father followed my advice and was indeed surprised. In the middle of this imaginative exercise, he suddenly felt as if the girl was stroking his forehead and smiling. "But father," she whispered, "don't worry. You loved me. That's the only thing that matters." The man was sure that this message was not just wishful thinking. He could still feel his daughter's fingers stroking his forehead. From that day on he stopped his tormenting himself with self-reproach.

A sincere apology, whether delivered to the living or the dead, is the key to healing.

People who have not divorced amicably should make up for this, at least in their imaginations. The lands of the spirit are broad. They do not stop at the border between here and there. They transcend space and time. We can send and receive information wirelessly in our physical world, but we are able to do so even more freely in the metaphysical world. When grief is combined with feelings of guilt, asking for forgiveness is the way to make amends. Will this request be heard? It is certainly worth a try. The judgments the living make about us are often wrong. Our fellow human beings have never been in our shoes and cannot fully understand our predicaments. However, those who are already travelled beyond the miniscule limits of earthly judgments can measure things by a more exact standard.

Pacification of anger

Sometimes people who have suffered misfortune refuse to grieve. Rather than allowing themselves to be led through the doorways of awareness described above, they invest their strength in a denial of what has happened or in a frantic search for a scapegoat. The latter only makes things superficially easier to bear. They believe their anger towards those who are allegedly responsible for their misfortune is an expression of the value they attach to what has been lost. But who can correctly assess the complex web of causes, especially when they are under severe emotional pressure? Nobody can. Unconscious transfers and projections occur – these are phenomena that have been well researched in psychology – but this does not justify them. Neither stands up to ethical scrutiny.

What is a transfer? Let's look at an example. A man is sad because he has been reassigned from outside work to office work, which he extremely dislikes. The reason for the reassignment is his advanced age, but he doesn't want to hear this. He attacks the head of department, who had no choice in the matter. In doing so, the man transfers his anger onto a person who is not responsible for the cause of his misfortune. Hospital doctors are used to such incidents. When patients die in hospital, doctors are often suspected or even insulted by the relatives of the deceased of having done their duty "sloppily". This is one reason why malpractice insurance is sadly essential these days.

Of course, a disaster *can* be due to another person's sloppiness, negligence, injustice, carelessness, or even spite. But no one can guarantee that they would have done any better in the other person's position. Think about how many mistakes we ourselves have already made – with minor consequences, thank God – and think about everything that could have gone wrong! Can we really condemn someone who has failed, in their weakness – with devastating consequences? Aren't we rather called to strive to be merciful, just as we, in a different context, would be dependent on mercy?

Now what is a projection? Like a transfer, it channels anger in the wrong direction. The psychological explanation is that the objectionable behaviour of people we don't like brings us face to face with something that we don't like about ourselves, the existence of which we have suppressed. This is the height of unethical frustration management! One is worried about a problem in oneself, does not want to admit that it exists, but fights against it by attacking others. An example of this would be a woman who has criticised and oppressed her husband for years. He is now in need of care, and he is in a care home. During her visits there, she berates the nursing staff for not caring well enough for her husband. Regretting her own failure, she projects her inner anger about it onto the innocent staff.

We should avoid allowing a tragedy to lead to a desperate search for scapegoats. The pain we feel is not lessened by lashing out and causing more pain. It does not make us more comfortable to know that others are also suffering or need to make atonement. And revenge is a lot less sweet than we think. It inevitably leaves with the bitter aftertaste of having sunk to the level of an offender.

As Viktor E. Frankl showed us, railing against fate and anger at those who might have caused the suffering can only be alleviated by deference to the mystery that hovers over every tragedy. Whatever can be gleaned from a reconstruction of the causes, there always remains something inscrutable. Why was there a flood in a mine? Because it rained heavily for weeks, because the tunnel structure was technically outdated, because a number of blasts were performed in succession ... There is no definitive, understandable cause for the death of a single miner. Things could always have turned out differently. He could have been sick or on holiday on the day of the flood. He could have happened to be safely in a side tunnel at the time the water broke in. The ultimate reason for his fate remains a secret. Blessed are they who can accept this with humility. They will find peace.

I was sitting with a sobbing student. She had recently learned that she was conceived by rape. Her mother, with whom she had grown up, had never mentioned her father; his name was not on her birth certificate. Recently, however, she had been thinking about tracking down her biological father, and her mother had told her the truth.

The young woman was shaken and sad. Her self-esteem plummeted. She had sudden doubts about her genetic inheritance. "Who am I?" she asked herself. "Do I have an inherent criminal streak?"

"Spiritually, you are a new person, unique and without equal on this earth," I assured her, quoting Viktor E. Frankl: "Parents pass on their chromosomes to their children, but they do not breathe the spirit into them." She accepted this argument. After a long conversation, we wrote a letter together to the unknown father of unknown whereabouts. "Father," wrote the student, her hand-writing erratic in her excitement, "wherever you may be, I hope that my soul may reach out to yours. Unfortunately, I know nothing at all about you except that you committed a

terrible crime. That's why I want to consider the possibility that you also have a good side, or that you have grown better and no longer commit violence. It is also possible that you are in prison, or dead.

This is what I want to say to you: I, your daughter, am not your judge. I hope for your sake that you regret your bad deed. If you do, it might help you to know that I am happy to be alive. Just as in nature, magnificent plants are fertilised by decaying matter and rotting carcasses become food for insects, something good has miraculously emerged from your crime, as a result of Mother's help and willingness to sacrifice herself. That doesn't justify what you did, but it should be a consolation for you in dealing with your guilt."

Consoling her father was the best possible consolation for the student herself in her crisis.

Acceptance of incapacity

A successful life consists of two complementary halves, represented here by two semicircles, one on the left and one on the right. The two semicircles match up to form a perfect circle; they depend on one another to complete the figure.

The semicircle on the left is a person with their skills, talents and experiences. It represents the totality of what this person has to give to the world: everything that they can contribute meaningfully and lovingly for the benefit of those around them. The experiences that can usefully be brought to bear may include traumatic ones. Most people who have experienced intense grief have a better understanding of other people's sorrows and understand them much more easily than people who have had no such experiences. Their ability to identify emotionally with such experiences condenses into a kind of experiential competence, acquired in the heat of pain, which, alongside any specialist knowledge they may have, authorizes them to approach similarly-wounded people with sensitivity.

The semicircle on the right is a piece of the world, part of the person's environment. Something neglected or imperfect, a part of reality that requires repair. As nothing in the world is perfect, this can be anything: a human, an animal, a plant, a mountain, a body of water, a building, a street ... It is simply a need that exists outside of the person. There are a lot of needs in our world: neglected children, homeless people, elderly people, broken families, helpless strangers, abandoned pets, polluted ponds, unfair contracts, run-down neighbourhoods, untranslated books, vulgar films – the list goes on and on. What every need has in common is that the meaning of the situation provides an urgent call for it to be filled.

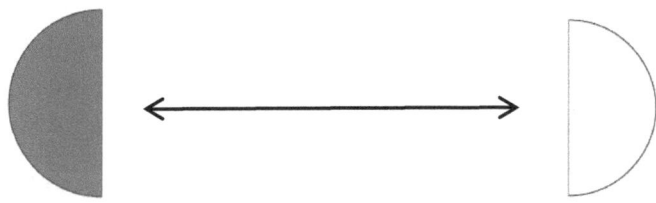

Think about it: who is able to meet a specific need? Only someone with the relevant skills. Children can be taught by a person who has pedagogical training. People who know multiple languages can translate books. This means that a specific semicircle on the right will not fit together with any old semicircle on the left, but only one that matches it. Or, to put it the other way around, we can assume that for every person and their skills (left-hand semicircle) there is a set of needs in the world (right-hand semicircle) that requests and invites them to dedicate themselves to it in a constructive way – *because they can*.

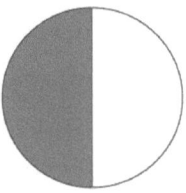

If this request is heard and obeyed, both sides are satisfied; the semicircles come together to form a complete and successful circle. The little bit of the world that requires repair is being put back in order. A person who contributes to this feels its importance and its meaningfulness to life. This is good for both sides.

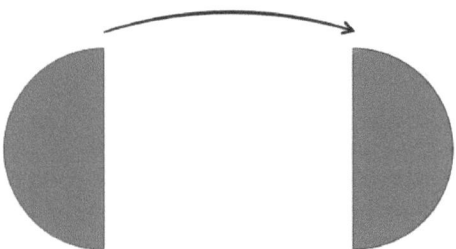

Sometimes, in grief, a person is involuntarily catapulted from the left to the right-hand semicircle. The person is no longer able to use their resources to make a positive change in the world; they have themselves become a part of the world that is in need of help, an opportunity for someone else to make themselves useful. As a baby or a young child, everyone is located in the right-hand semicircle, and is unaware of their incapability at that time. Later, in the case of significant physical or mental incapacity, senility or dementia, a person is often uncomfortably aware of this deficit. Many people in the right-hand semicircle feel they are a burden to others, and that their life has no meaning. Their relatives are just as sad, because they experience the disabled person's incapacity first-hand without being able to do anything about it.

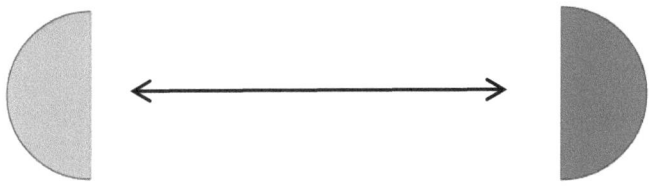

But there is not a more positive interpretation of the person's situation? They have not fallen out of the complete two-part picture of a successful life. They have simply become an invitation to others to fulfill a need instead of being the one who receives that invitation. They are now a living opportunity for others to care for them, and they thereby bring out the best in other people: love for others. To put it bluntly, one could say that people with diminished physical or mental capacities fulfill meaning by offering stronger and healthier people a meaningful chance to provide care.

If both sides understand their interaction in this way, grief teaches them both to be more aware of meaning. What is truly meaningful in life? The expensive car in your garage? Hardly. More likely, your partner teaching you how to drive. And what if this partner is now senile? The fact remains. Love is what has true value, not luxury. This value is far too often underestimated. Grief makes it clear.

A couple asked for my advice on a delicate matter. The wife, dressed in mourning, told me that her elderly mother, who had been bedridden for months, had just died. The problem was not the loss of her mother, which had been expected, but the decision as to whether her father should be informed of his wife's death. When I asked why he didn't know about it already, she gave me the following explanation:

The woman's parents were a "golden wedding" couple. When her mother became ill, her father took sole charge of her care and refused any additional help. Serving his wife had become his personal life's task. Three weeks earlier, however, he had been hospitalised following a heart attack. He was now in intensive care and things were not going well for him. It was unclear how aware he was of his surroundings, but according to his daughter and son-in-law, he indicated in between periods of unconsciousness that something was tormenting and troubling him. He would twist the wedding ring on his finger. This is why the daughter suspected that her father was struggling with the idea that he shouldn't be lying there in his illness because he was needed at home by his wife. Of course he knew that efforts would be made to look after her, but to him this was not the same as his own care, to which his wife was long accustomed.

It should be noted that it must have been very stressful for the woman to be separated from him, and she died immediately after he was admitted to the hospital. But, so far, this had been kept secret from him. Doctors had advised against telling him the bad news about his wife's death during his illness. Some were afraid that the shock would kill him. Others suggested that he would die soon anyway and that he should be spared this final pain.

The doctors' concerns were valid. Nevertheless, the symbol of the two semicircles suggests another consideration. The old man had lived a full life and brought up his offspring. He had fulfilled his professional duties, made it through difficult years, enjoyed good years, and in his later years he had sacrificed himself to care for his wife. He had lived out a valuable human existence, on which he could justifiably look back with pride. There was only one flaw: one task had not been completed. The circle wasn't completely closed. From his persepctive, there had been an interuption in his care for his beloved wife. As a result, anxiety may have crept into his heart and destroyed his inner calm, preventing him from dying in peace. The daughter knew her father well and sensed what was going on.

Thus I recommended that the couple should (contrary to medical advice) gently inform the father that his wife had gone on ahead of him, so that he no longer needed to worry about her. Hopefully, the old man would then see the last task he had set himself as complete and he would be able to shut his eyes with relief.

After a few weeks I received good news from the son-in-law. The old man had received the news of his wife's death very calmly. He nodded his head several times and whispered: "She's fine now ..." He lived on longer than had been expected, slept most of the time and from then on had a relaxed expression on his face. When he died, the fingers of his left hand clutched the wedding ring tightly. This ring had become a symbol of a circle of meaning in his life that had achieved a glorious completion.

Creation does not lose its dead

In 1995, Wilhelm Gräb wrote a famous sentence in a book he edited called *Big Bang or Creation* (1995): "Nature loses its dead, creation does not lose them." Since then, this idea has been taken up by a number of prominent thinkers (including Günter Ewald in his Bochum lectures). I dare not join their illustrious ranks. However, I would like to offer a few thoughts to the readers of this book.

The term "nature" here refers to all biological processes. Its principle is to recycle everything: water and all the organisms that came from it. For example, if a gazelle is killed and eaten by a pride of lions, the gazelle entity disappears into the lion entities. The gazelle is no longer a being in itself, although other creatures have absorbed its being. Similarly, a cloud disappears in the clearing sky once it has deposited its rain. The moisture in the cloud has not ceased to be – nor does the flesh of the gazelle – but that particular cloud no longer exists. The human organism is also subject to nature's recycling principle. It disappears into the dust from which new generations emerge. Thus, nature loses its clouds into streams, and its dead in order to form new living things – by many inscrutable detours.

What does the term "creation" refer to in the quote? One might say that it means a view of the world that includes the self-aware and meaning-oriented spirit created in "God's image", fused in personal union with a superbly complex organism. "Creation" includes what is human about people. In doing so, it transcends purely material biological principles, or couples them with the mystery of the spiritual. But since eternity – being beyond time and space – is one of the mystical qualities of the spiritual realm, and everything that decays and perishes can only decay and perish in space and time, the self-aware and meaning-oriented spirit of a person must remain identical with itself, never disappear and never be recycled by nature.

It remains completely itself. Creation does not lose its dead – the spiritual person.

Here's how the eminent scientist and Nobel Prize winner John C. Eccles arrived at the mystery after decades of research on the brain: "The self-conscious mind emerges as an identity-bestowing effect upon the material body ... It selects from a multiplicity of centres at the highest level of brain activity according to attention, and integrates its selection from moment to moment, thus imparting unity to even the most transient experiences ... it exerts a superior inter-pretive and controlling influence upon the neural events ... What happens in death? Then cerebral activity is finally stilled. The self-conscious mind now finds that the brain, which it has been exploring and manipulating so successfully throughout a long life, no longer gives any response at all. What then happens is the final question.[3]"

This final question is unanswerable. Or at best it can be answered with a negative statement, for example according to Viktor E. Frankl: "The person is nowhere in the room – not even in the brain – and not in the grave ..."

Can difficult thoughts like this help people to process grief? Perhaps. Nature designed creation for the development of life. Modern physics has discovered astonishing evidence for this. According to Hubble's law, our universe is expanding at great speed like a huge balloon. The development of galaxies and planets is very sensitive to the rate of this expansion immediately after the Big Bang: if this had been too slow, the universe would have collapsed before galaxies had time to form. Conversely, if the expansion had been faster, galaxies would also not have formed. The expansion would have "blown matter apart as a strong wind disperses fog" (Reinhard Breuer, astrophysicist in Munich). Adjusting the rate by as much as one part in a trillion in either direction might have made it impossible for any life to develop.

Another note: The two hydrogen atoms in a water molecule are not exactly opposite one another on either side of the oxygen atom, but at an angle of 104.5 degrees. If this angle were slightly different:

103 degrees or 106 degrees, say, water would not have the properties necessary for biological life, such as being able to rise dozens of meters in trees. There are many more examples like this.

We just have to believe that nature designed creation for life. And life culminates in the existence of a self-aware and meaning-oriented spirit. Why would the universe go to such trouble if everything was going to disappear again without a trace? No, our dear dead were wanted, fundamentally wanted, just like us living creatures. Creation, which has performed miracles for billions of years to bring us into being, will not let us fall into non-existence.

A living relic – in a poet's words

In his 19th century short story *A Living Relic,* the Russian writer Ivan Sergeyevich Turgenev masterfully described the dizzying heights of inner wisdom and heroic acquiescence in the face of incomprehensible fate, to which the human spirit can rise from the depths of sorrow. Let us have a look at his moving words (translations by Constance Granett)

On his foray through the forest, a hunter enters a half-open shed and discovers a small figure wrapped in blankets.

A head utterly withered, of a uniform coppery hue – like some very ancient holy picture, yellow with age; a sharp nose like a keen-edged knife; the lips could barely be seen – only the teeth flashed white and the eyes; and from under the kerchief some thin wisps of yellow hair straggled on to the forehead. At the chin, where the quilt was folded, two tiny hands of the same coppery hue were moving, the fingers slowly twitching like little sticks. I looked more intently; the face, far from being ugly, was positively beautiful, but strange and dreadful; and the face seemed the more dreadful to me that on it – on its metallic cheeks – I saw, struggling ... struggling, and unable to form itself – a smile.

Slowly, the hunter recognizes the strange figure as Lukerya, formerly the most beautiful of the court servants, the Lukerya who was always laughing, singing and dancing and after whom all the young boys were running. He sits down next to her, curious to know how she ended up this way. She tells him about her love affair with Vasily, and how she got up one night, thought she heard his voice and, following it, fell down the stairs.

'Ever since that happened,' Lukerya went on, 'I began to pine away and get thin; my skin got dark; walking was difficult for me; and then – I lost the use of my legs altogether; I couldn't stand or sit; I had to lie

down all the time. And I didn't care to eat or drink; I got worse and worse. Your mamma, in the kindness of her heart, made me see doctors, and sent me to a hospital. But there was no curing me. And not one doctor could even say what my illness was. What didn't they do to me? – they burnt my spine with hot irons, they put me in lumps of ice, and it was all no good. I got quite numb in the end ...

So the gentlemen decided it was no use doctoring me any more, and there was no sense in keeping cripples up at the great house ... well, and so they sent me here ...

'But this is awful – your position!' I cried ... and not knowing how to go on, I asked: 'and what of Vassily Polyakov?' A most stupid question it was.

Lukerya turned her eyes a little away.

'What of Polyakov? He grieved –he grieved for a bit – and he is married to another, a girl from Glinnoe. Do you know Glinnoe? It's not far from us. Her name's Agrafena. He loved me dearly – but, you see, he's a young man; he couldn't stay a bachelor. And what sort of a helpmeet could I be? The wife he

found for himself is a good, sweet woman – and they have children. He lives here; he's a clerk at a neighbour's; your mamma let him go off with a passport, and he's doing very well, praise God.'

In this extract we see a particularly courageous way of processing grief. The sick young woman is happy about her former lover's family bliss, even though she cannot be part of it. Her love for him is more powerful than the cruelty of her fate.

The next passage shows how little power she allows fate to have over her soul:

'And aren't you dull and miserable, my poor Lukerya?'

'Why, what is one to do? I wouldn't tell a lie about it. At first it was very wearisome; but later on I got used to it, I got more patient – it was nothing; there are others worse off still.'

'How do you mean?'

'Why, some haven't a roof to shelter them, and there are some blind or deaf; while I, thank God, have

splendid sight, and hear everything – everything. If a mole burrows in the ground – I hear even that. And I can smell every scent, even the faintest! When the buckwheat comes into flower in the meadow, or the lime-tree in the garden – I don't need to be told of it, even; I'm the first to know directly. Anyway, if there's the least bit of a wind blowing from that quarter. No, he who stirs God's wrath is far worse off than me.

Lukerya is realistic about her situation. But the reality is more multifaceted than it seems at first glance, as Lukerya recognises. Suffering has no limits. For every poor person there are even poorer people, and for every sad person there are even sadder people. Lukerya takes full advantage of this insight – if there are people poorer and sadder than her, then she still has reasons to be joyful, such as smelling the scent of the flowering trees.

What is she doing? She expands on her reasons to be joyful:

I look and listen. The bees buzz and hum in the hive; a dove sits on the roof and coos; a hen comes along with her chickens to peck up crumbs; or a sparrow flies in, or a butterfly – that's a great treat for me. Last year some swallows even built a nest over there in the corner, and brought up their little ones. Oh, how interesting it was!

She moistened her parched lips.

'Well, in the winter, of course, I'm worse off, because it's dark: to burn a candle would be a pity, and what would be the use? I can read, to be sure, and was always fond of reading, but what could I read? There are no books of any kind, and even if there were, how could I hold a book? [...] But even though it's dark, there's always something to listen to: a cricket chirps, or a mouse begins scratching somewhere.

The hunter can hardly believe her calm composure and asks about her loneliness. But it is precisely from the meditative silence into which she sinks that she draws her unperturbed affirmation of life.

I lie here sometimes so alone ... and it's as though there were no one else in the world but me. As if I alone were living! And it seems to me as though something were blessing me ... I'm carried away by dreams that are really marvellous!'

'What do you dream of, then, Lukerya?'

'That, too, master, I couldn't say; one can't explain. Besides, one forgets afterwards. It's like a cloud coming over and bursting, then it grows so fresh and sweet; but just what it was, there's no knowing! Only my idea is, if folks were near me, I should have nothing of that, and should feel nothing except my misfortune.' Lukerya heaved a painful sigh. Her breathing, like her limbs, was not under her control.

The young woman, who once had a superb voice, tries to sing a song to the hunter. It is too much of a strain and a tear glistens on her lashes. He dries them with a handkerchief, which he leaves for her as a gift, and her face reddens slightly. In return, she tells him about her dreams. In one dream, she sees herself running across a wide meadow to pick cornflowers, pursued by a vicious dog who prevents her from doing so. Suddenly a figure dressed in white reaches out and pulls her up. The dog has to let her go.

'Then only I understood that that dog was my illness, and that in the heavenly kingdom there was no place for it.'

Her dream reveals her basic trust, but also the remarkable (anthropological) insight that she as a person is more than her illness. She is able to distance herself from the "dog", which saves her from being psychically "eaten up" by it.

Lukerya adds another "dreamlike" thought: the idea of sacrifice. She has a vision of her dead parents visiting her in the shed and bowing deeply before her. She asks her mother and father why they are doing this.

"You have made an end of your own sins; now you are expiating our sins."

In other words, the woman extracts a clearly defined meaning from her seemingly senseless suffering by seeing it as a sacrifice for the salvation of her parents' souls. She doesn't want to lie there in misery for nothing.

At the end of her conversation with the hunter, the woman is completely exhausted. She coughs and moans. He asks if there is anything else he can do for her.

'I want nothing; I am content with all, thank God!' she articulated with very great effort, but with emotion; 'God give good health to all! But there, master, you might speak a word to your mamma – the peasants here are poor – if she could take the least bit off their rent!

They've not land enough, and no advantages.... They would pray to God for you ...

I gave Lukerya my word that I would carry out her request, and had already walked to the door ... She called me back again.

'Do you remember, master,' she said, and there was *a gleam of something wonderful in her eyes and on her lips, 'what hair I used to have? Do you remember, right down to my knees! It was long before I could make up my mind to it ... Such hair as it was! But how could it be kept combed? In my state! ... So I had it cut off ... Yes ... Well, good-bye, master! I can't talk any more.' ...*

Lukerya has drunk the cup of grief to the last drop: her magnificent braids were the last sign of her lost health, youth and beauty. And yet her only wish is to help the poor farmers in the region. Turgenev's "living relic" is a witness to the richness of heart that people can still muster in their grief.

Living in readiness for departure

Elisabeth Kübler-Ross advised her readers and fans to live "in readiness for departure". This advice was not just intended to lift the taboo surrounding death. It is a reminder to deal carefully with the people and goods entrusted to us.

It is a healthy exercise to walk through your home as though you had to say goodbye to it (for example because you were moving to a hospice). You might place your hand on a piece of furniture and remember when and with whom you bought it. You might caress a birthday vase, wedding china, a particularly treasured book or the sheet music you have often played on the piano. Consider the Persian carpet paid off in instalments, the embroidered curtains, the jewelry box. You can't take anything with you, but it was great that these things were there and made their contributions to your own personal development. Wonderful! Then you consciously let go of all these things, relinquish them to others in your imagination, perhaps strangers, who may have need for them– and feel a joyful lightness and freedom within yourself. Once you reach this point, you can "wake up" from the exercise and get back to business as usual.

You can also talk to someone close to you as if it were your last conversation with them. You will be amazed at the touching intensity of communication generated by this idea.

These exercises can be explained with the help of a parable: When you are born, you are given a basket, with which you can go for a walk through your garden to collect fruit. Of course, you can only pick or collect what is there. Some people are unlucky and only find unripe or worm-eaten fruit. Others are lucky with their harvest. What is important, however, is that the basket is intended for collecting and sharing the harvest. You might fill it with red-cheeked apples, eat some of them and pass half on to others to make room for some pears. Once the pears are in the basket, some of them might be given to the needy to make way for plums and nuts ... At the end of the walk, when all the fruit collected has been used, the empty basket is put back with thanks. The true harvest is not in the basket. The effort of collection and the kindness of distribution has brought it into eternity.

Living "in readiness for departure" means living without fear of death, despair and mental breakdowns. It means living with joy and sadness as they come, in the constant awareness of being able to participate in a transitory world in values that death cannot destroy because they come from a higher world. Living "in readiness for departure" means not wanting to grasp at things, not wanting to hold on to them, not over-loading your basket. People often say that if they could live their life a second time they would make many different decisions. Well, "living in readiness for departure" also means being as kind and generous the first – and only – time we live our lives as we would have liked to have been when the time comes to say goodbye.

Since we are talking about farewells, I would also like to leave a piece of advice for my readers, following Elisabeth Kübler-Ross' example. I feel compelled to bequeath something, especially to those who are in emotional distress, because my entire professional work has been dedicated to them. I know that in principle everyone in the universe is alone in their plight. Even professional help has its limits. But it is precisely when they reach their limits that people often sense an overpowering superhuman presence. So here is my bequest, a summary after more than 30 years of clinical therapeutic practice:

"Place no faith in a scientific utopia that can get things back on track using technology and pills! Technology and pills are inhumane if they are not accompanied by the spirit of love. Don't rely on the modern priesthood of psychologists and psycho-therapists and their promises of salvation! They are not able to provide it. Don't labour under the illusion that political, sectarian or other cunning leaders will solve your problems! They will mainly use you for selfish purposes. At the same time, don't give up and assume that everything is hopeless! True hope transcends what is attainable or unattainable in this world.

Instead, reflect on the powers of your own soul. As human beings, you are unique, and as such you resound (the Latin word "personare" means to sound through) with a harmony that expresses all the Creator's care for his creatures. You are fundamentally wanted, welcome and invited to help shape the future of the human community. Everything you need to fulfill your mission has been given to you. Nothing is missing, in spite of your weaknesses and shortcomings. It is enough for you to resonate with the harmony of tender care for everything that has been entrusted to you. If you devote yourself to taking care of something or someone else, your own worries become smaller.

Reflect on your family. You can have no peace in life if you are not at peace with those close to you. The family has diminished in our modern culture, but with a big heart it is possible to expand it a little. It might include a divorced partner, a distantly related cousin, a friend's son or a neighbour's wife. Be patient and forgiving when your family members make mistakes, and do not "cast the first stone." Practice listening, trying to understand, and reacting with restraint. Your inner distress, fear or conflict may be enormous, but a harmonious family atmosphere is the best healing environment for it.

I know that you are not evil, although at times you behave aggressively, even towards yourselves. You constantly want to defend, enforce, protect, or hide something. You don't need to. Just let go, you are protected! Do not cling to what is easy and comfortable, do not flee from what is difficult and uncomfortable, dare to embark on the adventure of what is good and noble. Open yourself to what each day offers, because each day is one of many days. Any of them can be your last. Consider this in your actions and in your conversations with other people, then you will choose your actions and words carefully.

And don't forget to be thankful, because nothing is deserved, everything is a gift – given for a limited time. If you will grieve for it when its time is up, then you should also appreciate it beforehand!"

Or is it the other way around: can we humans only truly appreciate something when we have grieved for it? Is this the deepest meaning of grief?

Only those who have seen the dark cloudscan ever measure the fullness of the sky's blue.

Only those who have stood all alone on the shore learn to ask where the bridges are.

Only those who have breathed loneliness can value the loud turbulence of festivals.

Only those who have passed through silent valleys of suffering can rejoice in the desert flowers.[4]

Works cited:

[1] S. 30: Deutsches Ärzteblatt, Volume 94, Issue 25, June 1997

[2] S.41: Man's Search for Meaning, p.139 German edition

[3] S. 69: Karl Popper and John Eccles, The Self and Its Brain: An Argument for Interactionism, Springer, 1977, pp 238-9

[4] S. 91: Translated from: Hermann Traub, „Trotzdem geliebt", Johannis-Verlag, Lahr 1995

Images: Cover, 13, 20, 24, 26, 29, 31, 43, 56, 66, 72, 83, 92:
©Bernhard Keller – info@bkeller.eu

Circle graphics: 57, 58, 59, 60 61, 62:
©Bernhard Keller – info@bkeller.eu

Images created with AI image generator: 9, 16, 36, 49, 87

LIVING LOGOTHERAPY

A publicaton series of the Elisabeth-Lukas-Archive

PSYCHOTHERAPY WITH DIGNITY
Logotherapy in Action

> **Authors:** Elisabeth Lukas, Heidi Schönfeld
> **1. Edition:** September 2021
> **ISBN:** 978-3-00-066694-0
> **e-Book-ISBN:** 978-3-00-066693-3

LOGOTHERAPY
Principles and Methods

> **Author:** Elisabeth Lukas
> **1. Edition:** September 2020
> **ISBN:** 978-3-00-066678-0
> **e-Book-ISBN:** 978-3-00-066679-7

MEANING-CENTRED PSYCHOTHERAPY
Viktor Frankl's Logotherapy in Theory and Practice

> **Authors:** Elisabeth Lukas, Heidi Schönfeld
> **1. Edition:** August 2019
> **ISBN:** 9783000636004
> **e-Book-ISBN:** 9783000642746

Zeitfracht Medien GmbH
Ferdinand-Jühlke-Straße 7
99095 Erfurt, Deutschland
produktsicherheit@kolibri360.de